IGNITE

RISE FROM WITHIN

ARAVIND HARIDAS

Made with ♥ on the Notion Press Platform
www.notionpress.com

Contents

Contents

Preface

A Personal Spark

Namaste, and welcome. If you're holding this book, it's likely because, on some level, you feel a stirring within you — a whisper of a desire for something more, something better. Perhaps you sense untapped potential waiting to be unleashed, or maybe you're navigating a landscape of challenges and seeking a guiding light. Believe me, I understand.

My own journey, much like yours, has been a tapestry woven with moments of exhilaration and periods of deep introspection. There were times when I felt like I was shining, confident and ready to take on the world. And then there were other times, perhaps more often than I'd like to admit, when self-doubt crept in, when social interactions felt like navigating a minefield, and when the path forward seemed shrouded in mist.

"Ignite: Rise from Within" isn't just a collection of theories or abstract concepts. It's born from a genuine desire to share the insights and strategies that have helped me and countless others navigate these complexities and step into a more empowered, authentic version of ourselves. This book is the distillation of practical wisdom, drawing from psychological principles, real-life experiences, and a deep understanding of the unique challenges we face in our interconnected world, particularly as young individuals finding our footing.

Whether you're in Mumbai, Melbourne, or Manhattan, the fundamental human desire to connect, to feel confident, and to live a life of purpose resonates universally. While this book is crafted with the Indian context in mind – understanding the rich tapestry of our culture and social dynamics – the principles within are designed to spark a fire in anyone seeking personal growth, regardless of their background.

This journey of self-improvement isn't about becoming someone you're not. It's about peeling back the layers of self-doubt and societal expectations to reveal the vibrant, capable individual already residing within you. It's about learning to harness your emotions, navigate social interactions with grace and confidence, and cultivate an inner strength that allows you to face any challenge with resilience.

This book wouldn't exist without the unwavering love and support of three incredible individuals who have been my guiding stars from day one. To my Mother and Father, this endeavor is a humble testament to the values you instilled in me, the sacrifices you made, and the endless belief you've always had in my potential. Your love has been the bedrock upon which my life has been built, and I dedicate this book to you with deepest gratitude and affection.

So, take a deep breath. Know that you're not alone on this path. "Ignite: Rise from Within" is your companion, your guide, and your cheerleader. Open these pages with an open heart and a willingness to embrace change. The spark of transformation is already within you. It's time to ignite it.

With warmth and encouragement,

Aravind Haridas

PREFACE

Acknowledgements

With profound gratitude, I wish to express my deepest appreciation to my

Mother and my Father. Your unwavering love, boundless support, and the

countless sacrifices you've made have shaped me into the person I am today.

You've been my first teachers, my constant cheerleaders, and my ultimate

source of inspiration. To my Brother, thank you for your invaluable, often

unseen, support. This book is a reflection of the values you instilled and the

belief you nurtured within me, brought to life with every available resource,

including the quiet enablement of Technology and AI. Thank you, from the

bottom of my heart.

    Ignite: Rise from Within
    By Aravind Haridas

Introduction: The Ember Within – Your Journey Begins Now

Think about a time you felt truly alive, brimming with confidence, and effortlessly connecting with those around you. Now, contrast that with moments when self-doubt gnawed at you, social situations felt awkward, or the path to your goals seemed impossibly steep. If you've experienced this spectrum, you're not just normal – you're human. And you're precisely who this book is for.

In today's hyper-connected, constantly evolving world, particularly for young individuals navigating the intricate dance of identity, career, and relationships, feeling a bit lost or overwhelmed is almost a rite of passage. The pressures of social media, the expectations of family and society, and the internal yearning for something more can often leave us feeling like an ember struggling to catch flame.

But within each of us lies an incredible, often untapped, power – a core of potential waiting to be ignited. "Ignite: Rise from Within" is your invitation to embark on a journey of self-discovery and transformation, designed to help you fan that inner ember into a roaring flame of confidence, connection, and purpose.

This book is a comprehensive guide, a roadmap to unlocking your hidden potential and transforming into the best version of yourself. We'll explore three vital parts of your being: your Core Transformation & Emotional Mastery, where you'll build an unshakeable foundation; your Social Mastery & Attraction, helping you navigate relationships and charisma with ease; and finally, Life Integration & Continued Growth, ensuring your transformation is sustainable and ever-evolving.

You'll discover practical, actionable strategies, drawing from powerful psychological principles like Cognitive Behavioral Therapy (CBT) and the science of manifestation. Each chapter is designed to not just inform, but to empower you with tools you can use immediately. This is not just about reading; it's about doing, evolving, and ultimately, igniting the extraordinary person you are meant to be.

The journey starts now. Are you ready to light your fire?

Part 1: Core Transformation & Emotional Mastery

CHAPTER I

The Inner Architect: Foundations of Self-Awareness

*Knowing yourself is the beginning of all wisdom." –
Aristotle*

*Imagine you're building a magnificent structure – a grand
house, a towering skyscraper, or even a simple, sturdy home.
Would you start by just throwing bricks together, hoping for
the best? Of course not. You'd begin with a blueprint, a solid
foundation, and a clear understanding of the land you're
building on. Your life, your very being, is that magnificent
structure, and self-awareness is your blueprint. It's the
foundational understanding of who you are, what drives you,*

and what truly matters to you. Without it, you're building blind, reacting to the world rather than shaping your own experience.

Many of us go through life on autopilot, driven by external expectations, ingrained habits, and unconscious reactions. We might chase goals that don't truly align with our desires, get easily triggered by situations we don't understand, or struggle to make decisions that feel right. This isn't a failure; it's simply a lack of a clear internal map. Being self-aware means holding up a mirror to your inner world, understanding your thoughts, emotions, values, strengths, and weaknesses without judgment. It's the first, most crucial step in any journey of transformation.

i. *The Echo Chamber of Your Mind: Understanding Your Thoughts*

Your thoughts are powerful. They shape your emotions, influence your actions, and ultimately determine your reality. But how often do you truly listen to them, not just as fleeting whispers, but as core data points about your inner landscape? Self-awareness begins with observing your thoughts. Are they mostly positive or negative? Are they empowering or limiting? Do they serve you, or do they hold you back?

This isn't about policing every thought, but rather becoming an observer. When a thought pops up — "I'm not good enough," or "I can't do this" — instead of accepting it as truth, you can simply acknowledge it: "Ah, there's that thought again." This creates a crucial distance between you and your thoughts, allowing you to question them. This practice is a basic tenet of Cognitive Behavioral Therapy (CBT), where we learn to identify and challenge unhelpful thought patterns.

Exercise: The Thought Journal. For the next few days, carry a small notebook or use a note-taking app. Whenever you notice a strong emotional reaction, or a recurring negative thought, jot it down. Don't analyze it yet, just record it. You might be surprised by the patterns you uncover.

v.   *The Symphony of Your Soul: Decoding Your Emotions*

Emotions are not enemies to be suppressed; they are messengers. Anger might signal a boundary crossed; sadness might indicate a loss; joy points to alignment with your values. But often, we're taught to ignore or dismiss our feelings, especially "negative" ones. True self-awareness involves leaning into your emotions, understanding their source, and recognizing their purpose.

This is not about being overwhelmed by emotions, but rather recognizing them without immediately reacting. For example, if you feel anger rising, instead of lashing out, you can pause and ask: What is this anger telling me? Was a boundary violated? Do I feel disrespected? This conscious processing transforms an impulsive reaction into an insightful moment. For many young people, especially in Indian households, expressing certain emotions might be discouraged, making this awareness even more crucial. Learning to identify and articulate your feelings, even just to yourself, is a massive step towards emotional maturity.

Exercise: The Emotional Check-in. Several times a day, simply pause and ask yourself: "What am I feeling right now?" Name the emotion. Don't judge it, just identify it. Notice where you feel it in your body. This simple practice builds your emotional vocabulary and awareness.

v. *Your Inner North Star: Discovering Your Values*

What truly matters to you? Beyond what your family expects or what society dictates, what are your non-negotiables? Your values are your core beliefs, your guiding principles that inform your decisions and define your purpose. Are they honesty, integrity, freedom, community, innovation, kindness, security, or adventure? When your actions align with your values, you experience a sense of congruence and fulfillment. When they clash, you feel internal conflict and dissatisfaction.

Many people feel adrift because they haven't explicitly identified their core values. They might pursue a prestigious career that brings no joy, or engage in relationships that leave them feeling empty. True self-awareness involves consciously identifying these values and using them as a filter for your life choices. This is particularly relevant in cultures like India, where collective values and family expectations often weigh heavily. It's about finding harmony between your personal values and your cultural context.

Exercise: Values Clarification. Make a list of 10-15 things that are most important to you in life. Then, narrow that list down to your top 3-5 non-negotiable values. How do these values show up in your daily life? Where are the gaps?

v. *Strengths and Shadows: Embracing Your Whole Self*

Self-awareness isn't just about what's "good" about you. It's about acknowledging your strengths – your natural talents, skills, and positive attributes – and your shadows – your weaknesses, insecurities, and areas for growth. Embracing both is crucial for authentic self-acceptance. If you only focus on your flaws, you'll be
paralyzed by self-doubt. If you only focus on your strengths, you'll lack humility and miss opportunities for improvement.

Understanding your strengths allows you to leverage them, to play to your advantages in career, relationships, and personal pursuits. Recognizing your weaknesses isn't about self-criticism, but about identifying areas where you can learn, seek help, or simply accept what is. This holistic view of self-empowers you to operate from a place of honesty and continuous improvement. Remember, no one is perfect, and true growth comes from understanding and working with your authentic self.

Exercise: SWOT Analysis (Personal).

v. *Strengths: What are you naturally good at? What do others praise you for?*

v. *Weaknesses: What do you struggle with? Where do you feel insecure?*

By becoming the architect of your inner world, meticulously drawing the blueprint of your thoughts, emotions, values, strengths, and weaknesses, you lay an unshakeable foundation. This self-awareness is your anchor, preparing you for the powerful transformations that lie ahead in "Ignite."

v. *Opportunities: Growth Accelerators. What favorable conditions or emerging possibilities exist externally that you can strategically leverage? These are elements—new skills, valuable connections, or shifting cultural landscapes—that can accelerate your personal progress and expand your achievements.*

v. *Threats: External Pressures. Conversely, what external challenges or unforeseen circumstances might test your design? Shifting social environments, unexpected life events, or sudden changes in your immediate world. Identifying these*

allows you to proactively fortify your structure, adapt your plans, and protect your long-term vision.

CHAPTER II

Emotional Alchemist: Mastering Your Inner World

The only way out is through." - Robert Frost

In Chapter 1, we began to map your inner landscape, identifying your thoughts and feelings. Now, it's time to move beyond mere identification to mastery. Imagine an alchemist, not turning lead into gold, but transforming raw, sometimes overwhelming emotions into powerful fuel for growth. This is the art of emotional alchemy: understanding your feelings, regulating their intensity, and consciously choosing how to respond, rather than simply reacting. This process is central to developing emotional maturity – the ability to navigate your inner world with wisdom and grace.

Many of us grew up learning to suppress emotions. "Don't cry," "Don't be angry," "Just get over it." While well-intentioned, this advice can be detrimental. Unexpressed emotions don't disappear; they fester, leading to anxiety, *resentment, or even physical ailments. Emotional alchemy teaches us that every emotion, even the uncomfortable ones, carries valuable information. The key is to decode that information and use it constructively.*

i. *The Power of Pause: From Reaction to Response*

When a strong emotion hit – frustration, anger, sadness, fear – our primal instinct is often to react impulsively. This can lead to regrettable words, rash decisions, or emotional outbursts. The first step in emotional mastery is cultivating the power of pause. This small gap between stimulus and response is where your freedom lies.

v. *The 5-Second Rule for Emotional Regulation: When you feel a strong emotion brewing, give yourself five seconds before you act or speak. In that brief moment, take a deep breath. Ask yourself: "What am I truly feeling?" and "What is the most constructive way to respond right now?" This simple pause can prevent a lot of emotional damage and allow for a more mindful response.*

v. *Deep Breathing: A fundamental tool from CBT and mindfulness. When stressed or emotional, your breathing becomes shallow. Deep, diaphragmatic breathing (breathing into your belly) signals to your nervous system that you are safe, calming your physiological response to emotion. Practice 4-7-8 breathing: Inhale for 4 counts, hold for 7, exhale for 8.*

v. *Cognitive Behavioral Therapy (CBT) for Emotional Reframing:*

CBT offers powerful techniques to understand how your thoughts, feelings, and behaviors are interconnected. Often, it's not the event itself that upsets us, but our interpretation of the event. By challenging unhelpful thought patterns, you can change your emotional response.

Let's say you send a text message to a friend, and they don't reply for hours.

v. *Automatic Negative Thought: "They're ignoring me. They don't like me anymore. I must have done something wrong."*

Resulting Emotion: Sadness, anxiety, self-doubt.
CBT Challenge: Is there another explanation? Maybe they're busy, in a meeting, or their phone died. Is this thought based on fact or assumption? What's the evidence for and against this thought?

v. *Reframe: "They haven't replied yet. They're probably busy. I'll check in later if I don't hear from them."*

Resulting Emotion: Calm, patience.

By consciously engaging in this reframing, you shift your emotional experience. This isn't about denial; it's about gaining perspective and choosing a more realistic and helpful interpretation. This is especially useful for managing social anxieties and navigating interpersonal relationships common among Indian youth, where overthinking social cues can be prevalent.

Exercise: The Thought-Emotion-Action Chain. When you experience a strong negative emotion:
Identify the Situation: What just happened?
Identify the Thought: What were you thinking?
Identify the Emotion: What did you feel? (Name it specifically: anger, sadness, frustration, etc.)
Challenge the Thought: Is this thought 100% true? What's another way to look at this? What would I tell a friend in this situation?
Reframe the Thought: Create a more balanced or realistic thought.
Identify the Action: How would you act differently with this new thought?

v. *The Spectrum of Self-Soothing: Healthy Emotional Outlets*

Once you recognize an emotion, what do you do with it? Healthy emotional outlets allow you to process feelings without letting them overwhelm you or resorting to destructive behaviors.

v. *Expressive Outlets: Journaling, talking to a trusted friend or mentor, creative activities like painting, writing, or playing music.*

v. *Physical Outlets: Exercise (a run, a workout, dancing), yoga, meditation, deep breathing exercises (as mentioned before).*

v. *Mindful Distraction: Engaging in hobbies, spending time in nature, listening to music, watching a calming movie. The key here is mindful distraction – not escapism, but a Start*

CHAPTER III

The Mindset Reset: Cultivating Unbreakable Confidence

"Believe you can and you're halfway there."
- Theodore Roosevelt

Confidence. It's often misunderstood, seen as an inherent trait some are born with and others aren't. But true, unbreakable confidence isn't about arrogance or a lack of fear; it's a deep-seated belief in your own capability, your worth, and your ability to navigate challenges. It's the quiet certainty that you can handle what life throws at you, even if you don't have all the answers right now. Without this core belief, even the most talented individual can be paralyzed by self-doubt, hesitating to speak up, pursue opportunities, or connect genuinely with others.

Think of confidence as a muscle. The more you exercise it, the stronger it becomes. The good news? You absolutely can cultivate it, regardless of your past experiences. This chapter will give you the tools to identify and challenge the limiting beliefs that hold you back, and to actively build a powerful, empowering mindset that propels you forward.

i.   Unmasking Limiting Beliefs: The Saboteurs Within

We all have them: those insidious thoughts that whisper, "I'm not smart enough," "I'll fail," "No one will listen to me," "I'm not attractive enough." These are limiting beliefs, deeply ingrained convictions that we accept as truth, even though they often have no basis in reality. They stem from past experiences, criticisms, or societal conditioning. For instance, in many Indian contexts, pressure to conform or avoid standing out might inadvertently foster beliefs that discourage individuality or bold ambition.

These beliefs act like invisible chains, holding you back from your true potential. The first step to cultivating unbreakable confidence is to unmask these saboteurs.

Exercise: Belief Detective.
Think about an area where you lack confidence (e.g., public speaking, approaching new people, pursuing a hobby).
What thoughts immediately come to mind when you think about that area? Write them down.
For each thought, ask: "Is this 100% true, always and in every situation?" "Where did I learn this belief?" "What would happen if I believed the opposite?"

v.   Challenge them: "Is there evidence against this belief?" "What would I tell a friend who had this thought?"

You'll often find that your limiting beliefs are based on old information or fear, not current reality. Just like in CBT, questioning these thoughts is vital.

v.   *The Power of Affirmations: Speaking Your New Reality*

Once you've identified and challenged a limiting belief, you need to replace it with an empowering one. This is where affirmations come in. Affirmations are positive, present-tense statements that you repeat to yourself to rewire your subconscious mind. They work by consistently feeding your brain new, positive programming, gradually shifting your inner dialogue from self-doubt to self-belief.

v.   *How to Craft Powerful Affirmations:*

Present Tense: "I am confident," not "I will be confident."
Positive: "I am capable," not "I am not insecure."
Personal: Use "I" statements.
Specific (if possible): "I am a confident public speaker," rather than just "I am confident."
Emotional: Connect to the feeling. Say it like you mean it.

Exercise: Daily Affirmation Ritual.
Choose 3-5 affirmations that directly counter your limiting beliefs (e.g., if you thought "I'm not smart enough," your affirmation could be "I am intelligent and capable of learning anything").
Write them down.
Repeat them aloud (or silently with conviction) for 5 minutes every morning and every night. Feel the words. Visualize them becoming true. Consistency is key.

v. *Manifestation: Visualizing Your Confident Self into Being*

Beyond words, visualization is a potent tool for manifestation. Your brain doesn't always distinguish between what's real and what you vividly imagine. By consistently visualizing yourself as a confident, capable individual, you create a mental blueprint that your subconscious mind then works to bring into reality.

The Confident You Visualization:

Find a quiet place where you won't be disturbed. Close your eyes.

Take three deep breaths, relaxing your body.

Now, vividly imagine yourself in a situation where you currently lack confidence (e.g., giving a presentation, meeting new people, speaking to someone you admire).

See yourself acting with complete confidence. Notice your posture, your facial expression, the sound of your voice.

Feel the emotions associated with that confidence: calmness, self-assurance, joy, ease.

v. *Imagine the positive outcome: people listening, connections being made, success achieved.*

Hold this image and feeling for 5-10 minutes. Do this daily.

This practice primes your mind and body to perform confidently when you encounter similar situations in real life. It reduces anxiety and builds familiarity with the desired state.

v. *Small Wins, Big Confidence: The Action-Confidence Loop*

Confidence isn't just an internal state; it's also built through action. Taking small, manageable steps that push you slightly outside your comfort zone creates a positive feedback loop. Each small success reinforces your belief in yourself, making the next step a little easier. This is the Action-Confidence Loop.

v.   *The "Micro-Challenge" Approach:*

Identify one small action you can take today that requires a tiny bit of confidence.

Examples: Make eye contact with five strangers and smile. Ask a question in a meeting. Start a conversation with someone new in your class or workplace. Order something new at a restaurant. Offer a compliment.

Do it.

Acknowledge your success, no matter how small. "I did it! That felt good."

Each successful micro-challenge adds a brick to your confidence wall. Over time, these small bricks build an unbreakable fortress of self-assurance. For Indian youth, this could involve initiating a conversation with a relative you usually don't speak to, volunteering for a presentation at school, or expressing an opinion respectfully in a group discussion.

Cultivating unbreakable confidence is an ongoing journey, not a destination. It's about consistently challenging limiting beliefs, actively programming your mind for success, and taking courageous, small steps forward. As you become more confident in your abilities, you'll find that your entire world begins to expand, opening doors to new opportunities and deeper connections. The foundation is set; now, let's learn how to conquer the unseen forces that can slow you down.

CHAPTER IV

Beyond the Wall: Conquering Procrastination & Activating Your Drive

"The secret of getting ahead is getting started." - Mark Twain

We've all been there: staring at a task – whether it's studying for an exam, starting a new project, making that difficult phone call, or even cleaning your room – and feeling an invisible wall rise between you and the action. That wall is procrastination. It's not laziness; it's often a complex interplay of fear, perfectionism, overwhelming feelings, or a lack of clarity. When you delay tasks, you're not just postponing work; you're eroding your confidence, increasing anxiety, and hindering your momentum. The good news? That wall isn't impenetrable. You have the tools to break through it and activate your drive.

Understanding the Procrastination Loop: What's Really Going On?

Procrastination often isn't about avoiding the task itself, but avoiding the negative emotions associated with it – fear of failure, fear of judgment, boredom, discomfort, or feeling overwhelmed. Our brains are wired to seek pleasure and avoid pain, so when a task feels painful (even if it's just the discomfort of starting), we instinctively push it away. This provides temporary relief, but long-term regret.

i. *The Loop:*

Task appears daunting/unpleasant.
You feel negative emotions (anxiety, dread, overwhelm).
You avoid the task (distraction, delay).
Temporary relief.
Long-term guilt, stress, decreased confidence.
Next task feels even more daunting.
Breaking this loop requires understanding its components and applying targeted strategies.

v. *The "Chunking" Method: Making the Monster Managable*

One of the biggest triggers for procrastination is feeling overwhelmed. A large task seems like an insurmountable mountain. The solution is to chunk it down into smaller, more digestible steps. This makes the task less intimidating and provides clear starting points.

Example: "Write a report" becomes:
Outline main sections.
Research for Section 1.

Write Introduction.
Write Section 1 draft.
(And so on.)

Exercise: The Smallest Next Step. Take one task you've been procrastinating on. What is the absolute smallest, easiest first step you can take right now? Something so small it feels almost silly to avoid. For example, instead of "study for exams," it might be "open the textbook to the first chapter." Instead of "clean room," it might be "put one item away." Committing to just this tiny step dramatically lowers the barrier to starting.

v.   *The "Two-Minute Rule": Eliminate Friction*

Inspired by author James Clear, this rule is powerful: If a task takes less than two minutes, do it immediately. This applies to so many small things that build up and become mentally burdensome: replying to an email, washing a dish, making your bed, putting clothes away. By eliminating these minor frictions, you reduce mental clutter and build momentum.

v.   *CBT for Procrastination: Challenging Your Inner Excuses*

Procrastination is often fueled by unhelpful thoughts. Just like we learned in Chapter 2, Cognitive Behavioral Therapy (CBT) helps us identify and challenge these thoughts.

v.   *Common Procrastination Thoughts & CBT Challenges:*

Thought: "I need to feel motivated to start."

Challenge: "Motivation often follows action, it doesn't always precede it. What's one tiny thing I can do without feeling motivated?"

Thought: "This task is too hard/boring."

Challenge: "Is it truly all hard/boring, or just parts? Can I break it down? What's the smallest, most tolerable part I can start with?"

Thought: "I work best under pressure."

Challenge: "Does that mean I do my best work, or just any work? What's the cost of that pressure (stress, lower quality, missed opportunities)?"

Thought: "I'll do it later."

Challenge: "When exactly is 'later'? What am I avoiding by saying 'later'? What will be the consequence if I keep delaying?"

By consciously questioning these internal narratives, you strip procrastination of its power.

v. *Activation Energy: Creating a Starting Ritual*

Just like a rocket needs a burst of energy to leave the launchpad, you can create "activation energy" for yourself. A starting ritual can

signal to your brain that it's time to focus. This can be anything: making a cup of tea, putting on specific focus music, setting a timer for 25 minutes (Pomodoro Technique), or simply opening the relevant software.

Exercise: Your "Go" Signal. What's a small, consistent action you can take right before you start a task you tend to procrastinate on? Design your own ritual and commit to it. This primes your brain for focus.

v.   *The "Future You" Strategy: Leveraging Empathy*

Procrastination is often a battle between your present self (seeking comfort) and your future self (desiring accomplishment). Build empathy for your future self. Imagine how relieved, accomplished, or less stressed Future You will be if Present You just gets started.

v.   *Visualize the Relief: Close your eyes and imagine the task is done. How do you feel? What are the benefits? Hold onto that feeling. Now, imagine not doing the task. How do you feel then? Use the contrast to motivate yourself. This is a form of manifestation – manifesting the relief and success of completion.*

Conquering procrastination isn't about becoming a robot; it's about understanding your human tendencies and strategically redirecting them. By breaking tasks down, challenging unhelpful thoughts, creating strong starting rituals, and acting with empathy for your future self, you can consistently bypass the wall of delay and ignite your unstoppable drive. This newfound momentum will be crucial as we move into fueling your physical self.

CHAPTER V

Physical Ignite: Fueling Your Body, Powering Your Mind

Take care of your body. It's the only place you have to live."
- Jim Rohn

You've started building your inner fortress of self-awareness and confidence, and you're learning to conquer the insidious habit of procrastination. Now, it's time to bring your physical self into alignment with this powerful internal transformation. Your body isn't just a vessel; it's the engine that powers your thoughts, fuels your emotions, and enables your actions. Neglecting it is like trying to drive a high-performance car with a sputtering engine and stale fuel – you won't get far, or effectively. Physical Ignite is about understanding the profound, often underestimated, link between your physical well-being and your mental and emotional strength.

In India, there's a deep cultural appreciation for well-being, often expressed through traditional practices like Yoga and Ayurveda. This chapter aims to bridge traditional wisdom with modern

science, showing how simple, consistent physical habits can dramatically boost your energy, focus, mood, and overall confidence.

i. The Energetic Triad: Sleep, Nutrition, and Movement

These three pillars are non-negotiable for peak performance, mental clarity, and sustained energy. Think of them as the primary fuels your engine needs.

v. Sleep: Your Brain's Recharge Cycle.

In our fast-paced world, especially with academic and social pressures, sleep is often the first thing sacrificed. But sleep isn't a luxury; it's a biological necessity. During sleep, your brain consolidates memories, processes emotions, and clears out toxins. Lack of sleep leads to poor concentration, irritability, increased stress, and a weakened immune system.

The Power of 7-9 Hours: Aim for 7-9 hours of quality sleep per night.

Exercise:

v. Create a Sleep Sanctuary.

- Consistency: Go to bed and wake up at roughly the same time each day, even on weekends.
- Darkness: Ensure your room is as dark as possible (use blackout curtains if needed).
- Cool Temperature: A cooler room (around 18-20°C) is ideal for sleep.

v. Screen Time: Avoid screens (phones, laptops, TVs) for at least an hour before bed. The blue light suppresses melatonin, the sleep hormone.

v. Wind-Down Routine: Develop a relaxing pre-sleep ritual: read a physical book, listen to calm music, meditate, or take a warm bath.

v. Nutrition: Fueling for Performance, Not Just Pleasure.

What you eat directly impacts your mood, energy levels, and cognitive function. A diet high in processed foods, sugar, and unhealthy fats can lead to energy crashes, brain fog, and increased inflammation. A balanced diet, rich in whole foods, provides sustained energy and clarity.

The Indian Diet Advantage: Traditional Indian diets, emphasizing fresh vegetables, legumes, whole grains, and spices, are inherently nutritious. Focus on these foundational elements.

Exercise:

v. Mindful Eating for Energy.

- Hydration: Drink plenty of water throughout the day. Often, what feels like hunger is actually thirst.
- Balanced Meals: Include a mix of complex carbohydrates (whole grains, vegetables), lean protein

(dal, paneer, chicken, fish), and healthy fats (nuts, seeds, ghee in moderation) in every meal.

- Limit Processed Foods & Sugar: These provide quick energy spikes followed by crashes. Opt for natural sugars from fruits.
- Portion Control: Eat until satisfied, not stuffed. Listen to your body's hunger cues.
- Nutrient-Dense Snacks: Carry fruits, nuts, or seeds to avoid unhealthy snacking.

v. Movement: The Ultimate Mood Booster & Stress Reliever.

You don't need to become a bodybuilder or a marathon runner. Regular physical activity, even moderate, has profound benefits for your physical and mental health. It reduces stress, improves mood (through endorphin release), boosts cognitive function, and enhances body confidence.

Beyond the Gym: This isn't just about structured workouts. It's about incorporating movement into your daily life.

Exercise:

v. Find Your Flow.

- Daily Movement: Aim for at least 30 minutes of moderate-intensity activity most days of the week. This could be brisk walking, cycling, dancing, playing a sport, or doing yoga.

- Strength & Flexibility: Incorporate some form of strength training (bodyweight exercises are great) and flexibility (stretching, yoga) to build a resilient body.
- Make it Enjoyable: Choose activities you genuinely enjoy. If it feels like a chore, you won't stick to it. Explore traditional Indian forms like Surya Namaskar (Sun Salutations) which offer a complete mind-body workout.
- Micro-Breaks: If you have a sedentary job/study, take short breaks every hour to stretch, walk around, or do a few squats.
- The Mind-Body Connection: Listening to Your Vessel

Physical Ignite is ultimately about tuning into your body's signals. Are you feeling sluggish? You might need more sleep or better nutrition. Are you stressed? Movement can be an incredible release. Your body is constantly communicating with you. Learning to listen to it and respond with nourishing habits is a powerful form of self-care and self-respect.

By consistently fueling your body with adequate sleep, nutritious food, and regular movement, you're not just building physical strength; you're cultivating mental resilience, emotional stability, and an undeniable aura of vitality. This robust physical foundation is essential for truly owning your space and engaging with the social world we'll explore next.

Part 2: Social Mastery & Attraction

CHAPTER VI

Charisma Unleashed: The Art of Magnetic Presence

"Charisma is not a gift, it's a habit." – Unknown

You've built a strong inner core – self-aware, emotionally intelligent, confident, driven, and physically energized. Now, it's time to project that powerful internal state outwards. This is where Charisma Unleashed comes in. Charisma isn't a mystical quality reserved for a select few; it's a learned art, a set of habits that make you genuinely attractive to others, drawing them in not just romantically, but socially and professionally. It's about having a magnetic presence that makes people feel comfortable, engaged, and uplifted in your company.

In Indian society, where community and personal relationships are highly valued, charisma takes on an even deeper meaning. It's not just about superficial charm, but about being a person of warmth, respect, and genuine connection.

The Pillars of Magnetic Presence: Beyond Just Looks

True charisma is a blend of several key elements, most of which are cultivated from your inner work.

i. Authenticity: Your Unique Signal.

The most charismatic people aren't trying to be someone else; they are unapologetically themselves. Authenticity means aligning your internal state with your external expression. People can sense when you're being genuine, and it builds trust and rapport. Trying to mimic someone else's personality often comes across as forced or inauthentic.

Exercise:

v. Embrace Your Quirks. What makes you uniquely you? Your specific sense of humor, your unusual hobbies, your unique perspective. Instead of hiding these, find ways to subtly express them. This is where your individuality shines.

v. Presence: Being Here, now.

In our distracted world, true presence is a rare commodity. When you are genuinely present with someone, giving them your full attention, they feel seen, heard, and valued. This is incredibly attractive. It means putting your phone away, *making eye contact, and actively listening without planning your next response.*

Exercise: The Focused Listener. In your next conversation, make it your sole mission to truly listen. Don't interrupt. Don't plan what you'll say. Just absorb. Notice the difference in the interaction.

v.   *Warmth & Approachability: The Open Door.*

Charismatic individuals emit warmth. They have an open body language, a genuine smile, and an inviting demeanor. They make it easy for others to approach them and feel comfortable in their presence. This isn't about being overly friendly with everyone, but about being genuinely amiable.

Exercise:

- *The "Open Body" Posture. Practice standing or sitting with open posture: shoulders back, chest slightly out, arms uncrossed, face relaxed with a slight smile. Notice how this subtly changes how people perceive you and how you feel.*

v.   *Enthusiasm & Passion: Contagious Energy.*

People are drawn to positive energy and genuine passion. When you speak about something you're excited about, your energy is infectious. It doesn't mean being loud or boisterous; it means conveying genuine interest and positive emotion.

Exercise:

- *Share Your Spark. Think of one thing you are genuinely passionate about. Practice talking about it with enthusiasm, even to yourself in a mirror. Notice how your energy shifts.*

v. *The Art of Non-Verbal Charisma: Speaking Without Words*

A huge part of charisma is communicated non-verbally. Your body language, eye contact, and vocal tonality speak volumes before you even utter a word.

v. *Eye Contact: The Window to Connection.*

Confident and charismatic individuals maintain appropriate eye contact. It signals honesty, attentiveness, and confidence. Too little can seem shifty or shy; too much can be intense. Aim for a comfortable gaze, breaking away occasionally to look at their features, then returning.

Exercise:

- *The "Confidence Gaze." Practice holding eye contact a little longer than usual with people you interact with daily (friends, family, shopkeepers). Notice your comfort level.*

v. *Smiling: Your Universal Invitation.*

A genuine smile is one of the most powerful tools for connection. It signals warmth, friendliness, and openness. A forced smile feels artificial.

Exercise:

- *The "Duchenne Smile." Practice smiling genuinely. A "Duchenne smile" involves the muscles around your eyes wrinkling (your eyes crinkle). It's a genuine smile that reaches your eyes.*

v. *Vocal Tonality: The Music of Your Voice.*

It's not just what you say, but how you say it. A confident, engaging voice is clear, has varied pitch (not monotone), and an appropriate volume. Speaking too softly can make you seem timid, while speaking too loudly can be abrasive.

Exercise:

- *Record Your Voice. Record yourself speaking for a few minutes. Listen back. Do you sound confident? Monotone? Too fast? Too slow? Practice varying your pitch and speaking with clarity.*

v. *Cultivating Your Charismatic Persona: A Continuous Journey*

Charisma isn't a mask you put on; it's an amplification of your authentic self. As you continue to work on your inner foundation – your self-awareness, emotional mastery, and confidence – your natural charisma will begin to shine more brightly. It's about practicing these habits consistently until they become second nature.

By unleashing your charisma, you become a person others naturally want to be around, listen to, and connect with. This magnetic presence is the gateway to superior communication and social fluency, which we will delve into next.

CHAPTER VII

The Master Connector: Superior Communication & Social Fluency

"The single biggest problem in communication is the illusion that it has taken place." -
George Bernard Shaw

You've ignited your inner fire and begun to project charisma. Now, it's time to become a Master Connector, someone who navigates social interactions with grace, confidence, and genuine impact. Superior communication isn't just about speaking well; it's about listening deeply, understanding non-verbal cues, adapting your style, and building meaningful rapport. Social fluency is the art of moving seamlessly through various social settings, making everyone feel comfortable, and leaving a positive, lasting impression.

In a collectivist society like India, where relationships are paramount, mastering communication is not just a skill – it's a pathway to deeper personal bonds, stronger professional networks, and greater overall life satisfaction.

The Foundation: Active Listening – The Underestimated Superpower

Most people listen to reply, not to understand. This is a fundamental error. Active listening is the superpower of master connectors. When you truly listen, you gather information, build rapport, and make the other person feel valued and understood.

Components of Active Listening:

i. *Full Attention:* Put away distractions (especially your phone). Give the speaker your undivided attention.
v. *Non-Verbal Cues:* Maintain appropriate eye contact, nod occasionally, and use open body language.
v. *Verbal Affirmations:* Use small verbal cues like "Hmm," "I see," "Right" to show you're engaged.
v. *No Interruption:* Let them finish their thought without jumping in.
v. *Reflect & Paraphrase:* Briefly summarize what they said to confirm understanding. "So, if I'm understanding correctly, you're saying..." or "It sounds like you're feeling..."
v. *Ask Clarifying Questions:* "Could you tell me more about that?" or "What do you mean by that?"

Exercise:

- *The "Listen First" Challenge. In your next few conversations, consciously make it your goal to understand the other person completely before offering your own thoughts*

Notice how much more you learn and how the dynamic shifts.

- *The Art of Conversation: Beyond Small Talk*

While small talk is a necessary entry point, master connectors know how to deepen conversations and make them engaging.
Open-Ended Questions: Instead of "Did you have a good day?" (yes/no), ask "What was the most interesting part of your day?" or "What's been on your mind lately?" These invite elaboration.

- *Finding Common Ground: Listen for shared interests, experiences, or opinions. Once you find a connection, explore it. "Oh, you're into photography too? What kind of subjects do you like to shoot?"*
- *Storytelling (Briefly): People connect through stories. Share short, relevant anecdotes about yourself or your experiences. Don't monopolize the conversation, but offer glimpses into your world.*
- *Injecting Personality: Don't be afraid to show your unique humor, perspective, or enthusiasm. Authenticity is magnetic.*

The "FORD" Method (for building rapport): This is a simple acronym to help you remember topics that generally lead to engaging conversations:

v. *Family (or friends, background)*
v. *Occupation (work, studies, passions)*
v. *Recreation (hobbies, interests, what they do for fun)*
v. *Dreams (aspirations, goals, future plans)*

Use these as gentle guides, not a rigid checklist.

Exercise:

- *Conversation Starters Bank. Prepare a few open-ended questions related to current events, hobbies, or general life*
- *experiences. Practice using them to initiate and deepen conversations.*

v. Non-Verbal Communication: Your Unspoken Language

Your body language speaks volumes. Master connectors are aware of their own non-verbal cues and can read others'.

v. *Posture: Stand tall, shoulders back. Projects confidence and openness.*
v. *Gestures: Use natural hand gestures to emphasize points, but don't overdo it.*
v. *Facial Expressions: Be expressive! Your face should reflect the emotion of the conversation. A genuine smile, a furrowed brow when someone is serious, etc.*
v. *Proximity: Respect personal space. In India, comfort with closer proximity might vary by region and relationship. Observe cues.*

v. *Mirroring (Subtle): Subtly mimicking someone's posture or gestures can build rapport, but do it naturally, not overtly.*

Exercise:

- *Mirror Practice. Practice different facial expressions and open postures in front of a mirror. Notice how they make you feel. Observe people's body language in social settings and try to decode their unspoken messages.*

v. *Adapting Your Communication Style: The Social Chameleon*

- *Social fluency means being able to adapt your communication to different people and contexts. You wouldn't speak to your professor the same way you speak to*
- *your best friend, or to an elder the same way you speak to a child.*

- *Observe and Adjust: Pay attention to the other person's pace, vocabulary, and formality.*
- *Empathy: Try to understand their perspective and emotional state.*
- *Cultural Nuances: Be aware of cultural differences in communication styles. In India, deference to elders, use of respectful language, and indirect communication in certain contexts are important.*
- *Overcoming Social Anxiety: Stepping into the Arena*
- *Social anxiety is a common challenge, especially for young people in new environments. Superior communication means taking steps to overcome it.*

- *Exposure Therapy (Gradual): Start with small social interactions that make you slightly uncomfortable and gradually work your way up. (e.g., compliment a stranger, ask a question in a group, initiate a brief chat).*
- *Focus Outward: Shift your focus from your internal anxieties to the other person. Ask questions, listen actively. When you're genuinely interested in others, your self-consciousness fades.*
- *Preparation, Not Perfection: You don't need a script, but having a few conversation starters or topics in mind can reduce anxiety.*

By becoming a master connector, you not only improve your interactions but also deepen your relationships,

expand your network, and unlock new opportunities. This skill is foundational for all social dynamics, including

understanding attraction, which we'll explore in the next chapter.

CHAPTER VIII

Decoding Her World: Understanding Female Psychology (Part 1)

"The highest form of knowledge is empathy." - Bill Bullard

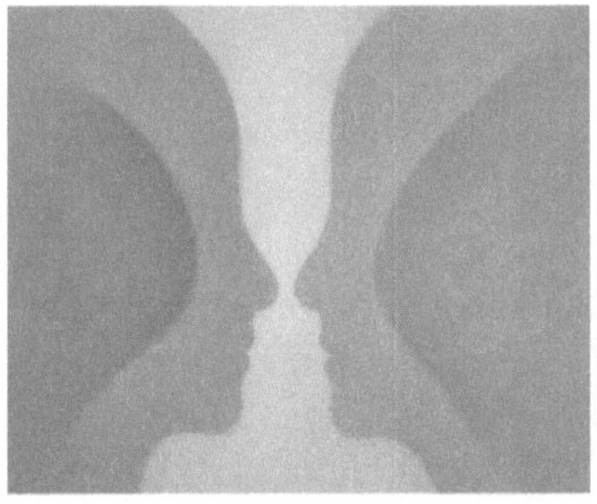

Now that you're building a strong foundation in self-mastery and general social fluency, it's time to delve into a specific and often misunderstood area: understanding female psychology. This isn't

about manipulation or playing games; it's about cultivating genuine empathy, recognizing nuanced communication, and building authentic connections based on mutual respect and understanding. This chapter is Part 1, focusing on foundational understanding and common pitfalls to avoid.

In India, societal norms and expectations can sometimes create a gap in understanding between genders. Traditional upbringing might not always equip individuals with the tools for open, nuanced communication across gender lines. This chapter aims to bridge that gap with respectful and insightful principles.

i. *Beyond Stereotypes: Recognizing Individuality*
v. *The first and most crucial rule: women are individuals. Just like men, they come from diverse backgrounds, have unique personalities, aspirations, and communication styles. Any generalization should always be taken as a broad tendency, not a universal truth. The goal is to develop sensitivity and adaptability, not to apply rigid rules.*
v. *Emotional Intelligence (EQ) is Key: Empathy Over Logic (Sometimes)*

While logic and problem-solving are valuable, emotional intelligence often holds more weight in female interactions, particularly in the initial stages of connection. Women often appreciate a partner who can:

v. *Listen and Validate: Instead of immediately offering solutions, listen to her feelings and validate them. "That sounds really frustrating," or "I can see why you'd feel that way." Sometimes, she just wants to be heard, not fixed.*
v. *Show Empathy: Try to put yourself in her shoes and understand her perspective, even if it differs from yours. "If I were in your situation, I think I'd feel similar emotions."*
v. *Understand Nuance: Women often communicate more subtly, using indirect language, tone, and non-verbal cues. Pay attention to how something is said, not just what is said.*

Common "Mistakes" (and how to avoid them):
These aren't "mistakes" in the sense of moral failings, but common missteps born from misunderstanding.

v.   *The "Fix-It" Reflex:*

Mistake: She shares a problem, and you immediately jump to offering solutions.
Why it's a mistake: She might just want to vent or feel understood, not necessarily get advice. It can make her feel unheard or that you're dismissing her feelings.
Instead: Listen first, validate her emotions, and ask, "Are you looking for advice, or do you just need me to listen?"

v.   *Ignoring Non-Verbal Cues:*

Mistake: Focusing solely on her words while missing her body language, tone of voice, or facial expressions.
Why it's a mistake: Non-verbal communication often carries more weight than verbal. A "fine" with a sigh means something entirely different from a cheerful "fine."
Instead: Observe her posture, gestures, eye contact, and vocal tonality. Ask yourself: "Does her body language match her words?"

v.   *Making Assumptions:*

Mistake: Assuming you know what, she's thinking or feeling, or what her intentions are.
Why it's a mistake: Leads to miscommunication and resentment. Everyone is different.
Instead: Ask clarifying questions. "When you said X, did you mean Y?" Or "I'm sensing you might be feeling Z, is that

right?"

v.   *Lack of Emotional Vulnerability (from you):*

Mistake: Always staying guarded, never sharing your own feelings or vulnerabilities.

Why it's a mistake: It creates a one-sided dynamic and prevents true intimacy. Connection thrives on mutual openness.

Instead: Practice healthy emotional vulnerability. Share appropriate feelings and experiences. This builds trust.

v.   *Not Understanding the "Test" (Subtle Challenges):*

Mistake: Misinterpreting a playful challenge or a subtle question about your boundaries as a sign of disinterest or an attack.

Why it's a mistake: People (not just women) sometimes "test" others to see if they are consistent, confident, and have boundaries. It's often unconscious.

Instead: Maintain your composure, stick to your values, and respond with humor or calm confidence. For instance, if she playfully teases you, respond with a confident smile and a witty retort, rather than getting defensive. This shows you're grounded.

Building Trust and Safety: The Foundation of Connection
For any deep connection to flourish, especially with women, a sense of trust and emotional safety is paramount.

v.   *Consistency: Be consistent in your words and actions. Reliability is attractive.*

v.   *Respect: Show genuine respect for her thoughts, opinions, and boundaries.*

v.   *Integrity: Be true to your word. Do what you say you'll do.*

v.   *Non-Judgmental Space: Create an environment where she feels she can be herself without fear of judgment or criticism.*

v.   *Confidentiality: If she confides in you, keep it private.*

Understanding these foundational aspects of female psychology – focusing on empathy, avoiding common pitfalls, and building trust – sets the stage for genuine connection. In the next chapter, we'll

move from understanding to actionable strategies for sparking and building authentic attraction.

CHAPTER IX

The Attraction Playbook: Sparking Genuine Connection (Part 2)

"The best way to predict the future is to create it."
- Peter Drucker

In Chapter 8, , *we laid the groundwork by focusing on understanding female psychology, emphasizing empathy and avoiding common missteps. Now, in Part 2, we shift gears to the Attraction Playbook – a set of actionable strategies designed to spark genuine connection and build chemistry. This isn't about tricks or manipulation; it's about intelligently applying the self-mastery you've cultivated to create an authentic, magnetic presence that naturally draws others to you.*

Remember, attraction is multifaceted. It's not just about looks; it's about personality, confidence, communication, and how you make others feel. This playbook integrates principles of psychology and social dynamics to help you become a person who genuinely connects.

The Pillars of Genuine Attraction: It's Not Just About You
Attraction isn't a unilateral phenomenon. It's a dance, a mutual exchange.

High-Value Communication (HVC):

i. *Focus on Value: Your communication should aim to add value to the interaction, not just take. This means making her laugh, offering an interesting perspective, sharing a relevant story, or genuinely listening and validating her.*

v. *Confident Delivery: Speak clearly, with good vocal tonality (Chapter 6), and maintain eye contact. This projects authority and self-assurance.*

v. *Engage, Don't Interrogate: Ask questions that invite conversation, not just short answers. "What do you enjoy most about your work?" vs. "Do you like your job?"*

Exercise:

- *The Value-Add Challenge. In your next social interaction, consciously think: "How can I add value to this conversation?" Can you offer a unique observation, a humorous comment, or a thoughtful question?*
- *Demonstrate Social Intelligence (Social Proof):*

People are often drawn to others who are well-regarded and comfortable in social settings. This isn't about showing off, but about demonstrating your ability to navigate social dynamics with ease.

- *Engage with Others: Don't just focus on the person you're interested in. Interact positively with others in the group. This signals that you're socially adept and likeable.*

- *Comfort in Your Own Skin: Be comfortable alone, but also comfortable interacting. Your ability to be at ease in various social scenarios is attractive.*

Exercise:

- *Group Engagement. When in a group, make an effort to include everyone in the conversation. Ask open-ended questions that allow multiple people to contribute.*
- *Vulnerability (Appropriate & Gradual):*
- *While confidence is attractive, a complete lack of vulnerability can be perceived as aloofness or insincerity. Sharing appropriate vulnerabilities creates deeper connection and shows you trust the other person.*
- *What to Share: Share a personal dream, a small fear, a past learning experience, or a moment of genuine emotion.*
- *When to Share: Build rapport first. Don't immediately overshare. Let it be a gradual process as trust develops.*

Exercise:

- *Share a Small Insight. In a comfortable conversation, share a brief, non-heavy personal insight or a mild insecurity you've overcome. Notice how it creates a connection.*
- *Playfulness & Teasing (Calibrated):*

Humor, as we'll discuss more in Chapter 11, is a powerful tool. Playful teasing, when done correctly, can build rapport and create a fun, dynamic interaction.

Key Rules:

It must be playful, not mean-spirited. The goal is to make them smile, not feel defensive.

Tease up, not down. Tease about things that show confidence (e.g., her being "too perfect" or a playful exaggeration), never about insecurities.

It must be followed by warmth. A playful tease should always be followed by a smile, a warm tone, or a compliment.

Example: "You're clearly the most organized person here, I bet your room is spotless... unlike mine!" (said with a playful smile).

Exercise:

- *Playful Observation. Practice making light, playful observations about a situation or a shared experience (not the person directly at first) to inject humor.*
- *Confident Initiation & Escalation:*
- *Attraction often requires someone to take the lead. This means initiating conversations, suggesting activities, and escalating the level of connection (from casual chat to deeper topics, from social interaction to asking for a number/date).*
- *Initiation: A simple "Hi, I'm [Your Name]" with a smile and eye contact is powerful. Follow up with an open-ended question.*
- *Escalation: If the conversation is flowing well, transition from general topics to more personal ones. "That's interesting, what truly motivates you?"*

The "Ask": If you feel a genuine connection, confidently ask for her number or suggest getting coffee/tea. Frame it as a natural progression of the enjoyable conversation. "I'm really enjoying talking to you, I'd love to continue this sometime. Can

I get your number?"

Exercise:

- *The Confident Ask. Mentally rehearse asking for a number or suggesting a casual meet-up. Focus on confident posture, direct eye contact, and a relaxed smile.*
- *Beyond the Initial Spark: The Long Game*

Attraction isn't a one-time event; it's a continuous process. The principles of authenticity, respect, and adding value are not just for the initial interaction but for building lasting, genuine connections. This playbook emphasizes that attraction is about becoming the kind of person who is genuinely interesting, respectful, and engaging, rather than relying on superficial tactics.

By mastering these elements of the Attraction Playbook, you empower yourself to spark genuine connections, build rapport, and navigate the exciting world of relationships with confidence and authenticity. This leads naturally into sustaining that interest and charm, which we cover in the next chapter.

CHAPTER X

The Modern "Playmaker": Beyond Attraction – Sustaining Interest & Charm

"The best way to keep a relationship is to never stop showing them why they chose you in the first place."
– Unknown

You've mastered the art of sparking attraction and initiating connections. But what happens after the initial spark? How do you move beyond fleeting moments to build sustained interest, maintain charm, and foster deeper, more meaningful relationships? This is the realm of The Modern "Playmaker" – someone who understands that true connection is an ongoing endeavor, a continuous investment in mutual growth and joy. This chapter focuses on the strategies that keep the flame alive, whether in nascent connections or established relationships.

In the Indian context, where long-term relationships (be it friendships, familial bonds, or romantic partnerships) are highly valued, the ability to sustain interest and build enduring charm is crucial for social and personal fulfillment.

i. *The Art of Continued Engagement: Nurturing the Connection*

The "chase" might be over, but the journey of discovery and connection continues.

Consistent Effort, Not Constant Contact:

Mistake: Bombarding someone with messages or calls, or going completely silent after the initial spark.

Instead: Be consistent with your outreach, but allow for space. A thoughtful message every few days, a call to genuinely check in, or planning a next meet-up shows interest without being overwhelming. Quality over quantity.

v. *Shared Experiences & Novelty:*

Why it works: Novel experiences release dopamine, creating positive associations. Shared activities build memories and strengthen bonds.

Instead: Don't fall into a routine too quickly. Suggest new activities, explore different places (even local hidden gems), or try new hobbies together. This keeps the relationship fresh and exciting. In

India, this could mean exploring a new regional festival, trying a different cuisine, or visiting a lesser-known historical site.

v. *Active Listening & Follow-Through (Revisited):*

Why it's crucial: Show you genuinely care by remembering details. If she mentioned a presentation at work, ask her how it went. If she spoke about a family event, ask about it later.

Exercise:

- *The Memory Note. If you struggle to remember details, discreetly jot down a few key points after a conversation (e.g., her sister's name, an upcoming event she mentioned). Use these to follow up later.*

v.   *Compliments & Appreciation (Authentic):*

Why it works: Everyone appreciates genuine compliments. Focus on specific qualities you admire – her intelligence, kindness, humor, resilience, or a particular skill.
Avoid: Generic or purely physical compliments. Make them specific and heartfelt.
Exercise:

- *Thoughtful Compliments. Make a habit of noticing specific positive traits in people you interact with. Practice articulating them genuinely. "I really admire how you handle challenges with such calm."*

v.   *Maintaining Your Own "Spark": Don't Lose Yourself*

True charm comes from being a well-rounded, interesting individual. Don't let your self-improvement journey stop once a connection is established.

v.   *Maintain Your Hobbies & Passions:*

Why it's important: Your passions make you interesting and give you things to talk about. Don't abandon your own life for another person.

Instead: Continue to pursue your interests. This maintains your individuality and gives you fresh experiences to share.

v.   Continue Personal Growth:

Why it's important: Stagnation is unattractive. Keep learning, keep challenging yourself, keep growing.

Instead: Read new books, learn new skills, reflect on your experiences. Share your insights.

v.   Manage Your Own Emotional State:

Why it's important: Your emotional well-being affects the relationship. If you're consistently stressed or negative, it will impact the dynamic.

Instead: Continue practicing emotional alchemy (Chapter 2). Seek healthy outlets for stress. Be a source of positive energy, not just a recipient.

v.   The "Little Things": Building Long-Term Charm

Charm isn't just about grand gestures; it's often built on the consistent execution of small, thoughtful actions.

Thoughtfulness: A   small   unexpected   gesture (remembering her favorite snack, sending a relevant article, a handwritten note).

Politeness & Manners: Basic courtesy, respect, and chivalry never go out of style. Holding doors, offering assistance, saying please and thank you.

v. *Humor (as we discussed in Chapter 11): Keep the laughter alive. Share funny observations or lighthearted banter.*
v. *Show, Don't Just Tell: Instead of just saying "I care," demonstrate it through your actions and support.*
v. *Respecting Boundaries: Understand and respect her personal space, time, and decisions. This builds trust and shows maturity.*

The Modern "Playmaker" understands that sustaining interest and charm is about continuous effort, authenticity, and a genuine desire to enrich the lives of those you connect with. It's about being a positive, growing force in their life, and never taking a connection for granted. This continuous growth mindset is crucial as we move to a powerful social superpower: humor and wit.

Part 3: Life Integration & Continued Growth

CHAPTER XI

Humor & Wit: Your Social Superpower

"A day without laughter is a day wasted." - Charlie Chaplin

You've built your inner core, mastered communication, and wield humor with finesse. Now, let's talk about one of the most powerful, yet often overlooked, social superpowers: humor and wit. Laughter is a universal language, a bridge that connects people, diffuses tension, and makes you instantly more likeable and memorable. It's not about being a stand-up comedian; it's about incorporating lightheartedness, cleverness, and an engaging spirit into your interactions.

In Indian culture, humor is often woven into daily life — from playful banter among friends and family to witty observations in conversations. Mastering this superpower can significantly enhance your social fluidity and deepen connections.

The Psychology of Laughter: Why It's So Potent

i. *Connection and Rapport: Laughter creates a bond. When two people laugh together, their brains release oxytocin, the "bonding hormone," fostering a sense of shared experience and intimacy.*

v. *Tension Release: Humor can defuse awkwardness, reduce stress, and break the ice in uncomfortable situations.*

v. *Perceived Intelligence & Confidence: Wit is often associated with intelligence and quick thinking. Someone who can make others laugh confidently is often perceived as more intelligent and secure.*

v. *Memorability: People remember how you made them feel. A shared laugh creates a positive, lasting impression.*

v. *Attraction: As discussed in Chapter 9, humor is consistently ranked as a highly attractive quality.*

Types of Humor: Find Your Style
You don't need to force a style that isn't natural. Experiment to find what resonates with you.

v. *Observational Humor: Commenting humorously on shared experiences or observations in the environment.*

Example: "This traffic is so bad, I think the cows are moving faster than us!" (in Mumbai traffic).

v. *Self-Deprecating Humor: Making light of your own flaws or minor mishaps. This shows humility and relatability.*

Example: "I tried cooking last night, and I think I successfully created a new form of charcoal." (Be careful not to overdo this, as it can sometimes signal low confidence if not balanced.)

v. *Wordplay/Puns: Clever use of language. Requires quick thinking.*

Example: "I'm reading a book on anti-gravity. It's impossible to put down!"

v. *Situational Humor: Responding humorously to something unexpected that happens in the moment.*

Storytelling (with a humorous twist): Sharing anecdotes from your life that have a funny resolution.
Developing Your Wit: Practical Strategies
Wit isn't something you're born with; it's a skill you cultivate.
Be Present & Observant: The best humor comes from paying attention. Notice details, absurdities, and unexpected connections in your environment and conversations.
Play with Language:
Word Association: Practice quickly associating words with other words or concepts.
Puns: While sometimes cheesy, practicing puns trains your brain for wordplay.
Exaggeration: Exaggerate a situation for comedic effect.
Practice Quick Thinking:
"Yes, And..." Game: In a casual conversation, respond to someone's statement with "Yes, and..." and add something creative or humorous. (e.g., "I'm going to the grocery store." "Yes, and watch out for the rogue shopping carts – they have a mind of their own!")
Respond with Questions: Sometimes a witty question can be more impactful than a statement.
Embrace Playfulness: Adopt a mindset that seeks out lightness and fun in interactions. Don't take everything too

seriously.

Collect "Material": Keep a mental (or actual) note of funny things you hear, see, or experience. These can be adapted for future conversations.

Learn from Others: Observe people who you find funny. What is their style? What makes them effective? Watch stand-up comedy or witty shows.

The "Dos" and "Don'ts" of Humor
DO:

v. *Be authentic: Your humor should feel like you.*
v. *Read the room: Understand your audience and the context.*
v. *Keep it positive: Aim to uplift, not put down.*
v. *Be self-aware: Know when your humor lands and when it doesn't.*

Smile: A smile can make even a slightly edgy joke land better.
DON'T:

v. *Be offensive: Avoid racist, sexist, homophobic, or otherwise discriminatory jokes. No one finds that attractive or funny.*
v. *Be mean-spirited: Don't use humor to belittle or mock others.*
v. *Overdo it: Not every sentence needs to be a joke.*
v. *Force it: If it doesn't feel natural, don't push it.*

Use inside jokes excessively: It can make others feel excluded.

Humor and wit are invaluable tools for enhancing your social interactions, deepening connections, and making you a truly memorable presence. By consciously cultivating your ability to bring laughter and lightness into your conversations, you unlock a social superpower that will serve you well in all aspects of your life. This playful confidence will naturally extend to your presentation, as we explore in the next chapter on image.

CHAPTER XII

The Image Architect: Dressing for Impact & Self-Expression

"Fashion is what you buy. Style is what you do with it."
– Unknown

You've built an incredible inner game, mastered communication, and wield humor with finesse. Now, it's time to ensure your external presentation reflects that internal strength. This is where you become The Image Architect – understanding that your clothing and grooming are not just about vanity, but powerful tools for self-expression, confidence, and making a desired impact. Your image speaks volumes before you even open your mouth, influencing how others perceive you and, more importantly, how you perceive yourself.

In India, where traditional wear often blends with modern styles, and cultural expectations around presentation vary, *understanding your personal style and dressing appropriately for different occasions becomes an even more nuanced art.*

Beyond Trends: Defining Your Personal Style

Forget chasing every fleeting fashion trend. True style is about understanding what looks good on you, what makes you feel confident, and what authentically expresses your personality.

i. *Understand Your Body Type:*

Certain cuts and styles flatter different body shapes. Research basic guidelines for your physique (e.g., V-neck for broader shoulders, straight cuts for height). This isn't about hiding flaws, but about enhancing your best features.

v. *Know Your Colors:*

Certain colors make your skin tone and features pop. Identify colors that truly flatter you. These will become your core wardrobe palette.

v. *Identify Your Personality & Lifestyle:*

Are you more formal or casual? Artistic or minimalistic? Your clothes should align with who you are and what you do. A corporate professional will dress differently from a creative artist, but both can be stylish.

v. *Quality Over Quantity:*

Invest in fewer, good-quality pieces that fit well and last longer, rather than many cheap, ill-fitting items. A well-tailored shirt from a good fabric will always look better than a wrinkled, mass-produced one.

v. *Indian Context: Embrace the versatility of Indian wear —*
   kurtas, Nehru jackets, traditional prints. These can be
   styled in modern ways for various occasions, blending
   tradition with contemporary flair.

Exercise:

• *Style Vision Board. Collect images of outfits, colors, and*
   styles that appeal to you. Notice common themes. What
   message do these styles convey? How do you want to be
   perceived?

The Impact of Fit: It's Everything!
This cannot be stressed enough: fit is more important than
brand or price. Clothes that fit well instantly elevate your
appearance. Loose clothes look sloppy; overly tight clothes look
uncomfortable and often unflattering.*

Key Areas for Fit:

v. *Shoulders: For shirts, jackets, and t-shirts, the shoulder*
   seam should align perfectly with your natural shoulder.
v. *Sleeves: Shirt sleeves should end at your wrist bone. Jacket*
   sleeves should show about half an inch of your shirt cuff.
v. *Trousers: Should break once over your shoes (unless you*
   prefer a no-break modern look). The waist should fit
   comfortably without needing a belt to hold them up.
v. *Length: Shirts should be long enough to tuck in but not so*
   long they bunch. T-shirts should hit around your hip bone.

v. *Tailoring is Your Best Friend: A good tailor can transform an average-fitting garment into something that looks custom-made for you. It's a small investment with a huge payoff.*

v. *Grooming: The Unsung Hero of Image*

v. *Your grooming habits are just as crucial, if not more, than your clothes. They reflect self-care, attention to detail, and respect for yourself and others.*

v. *Hair: Keep it clean, well-cut, and styled appropriately for your face shape and profession. Regular trims are essential.*

v. *Facial Hair: If you have a beard or mustache, keep it neatly trimmed and maintained. If clean-shaven, ensure a smooth shave.*

v. *Skin Care: A basic routine of cleansing, moisturizing, and sunscreen can make a significant difference. Clear, healthy skin boosts confidence. (This is increasingly relevant for men today.)*

v. *Hands & Nails: Clean, trimmed nails are a must.*

v. *Oral Hygiene: Fresh breath and clean teeth are non-negotiable for confident communication.*

v. *Fragrance: A subtle, pleasant scent can leave a good impression, but never overdo it.*

Exercise:

• *The "Head-to-Toe" Check. Before you leave the house, do a quick mental scan: hair, face, teeth, clothes (clean, pressed, fitted?), shoes (clean?), hands. This ensures you always present your best self.*

- *Dressing for the Occasion: The Context Matters*

Understanding the dress code and context is vital for making the right impression.

v. *Formal: Suits, traditional Indian formal wear (e.g., designer kurtas, bandhgalas).*
v. *Business Casual: Collared shirts, well-fitting trousers/ chinos, smart shoes.*
v. *Smart Casual: Jeans or chinos with a stylish T-shirt or casual shirt, sneakers or casual shoes.*
v. *Traditional: Kurtas, pyjamas, dhotis, etc., appropriate for cultural events or religious ceremonies.*

When in doubt, it's generally better to be slightly overdressed than underdressed. It shows you respect the occasion and the people you're meeting.

By becoming the architect of your image, you consciously align your external presentation with your internal growth. This isn't about superficiality; it's about leveraging your appearance to boost your confidence, enhance your social interactions, and project the powerful, refined individual you are becoming. This mindful approach extends to your digital presence, as we'll explore next.

CHAPTER XIII

Digital Presence, Real Impact: Leveraging Social Media for Personality Development

"In the digital age, your online identity is often as important as your offline one." – Unknown

In today's interconnected world, your presence extends far beyond face-to-face interactions. Your digital presence, particularly on social media, has become an undeniable part of your overall identity. It's not just a collection of posts; it's a curated reflection of your personality, values, and aspirations. Mastering this aspect means leveraging social media as a powerful tool for personality development, building your personal brand, and extending your positive impact, rather than letting it become a source of anxiety or distraction.

In India, social media platforms are incredibly pervasive, influencing everything from social trends to career *opportunities. Understanding how to navigate this landscape consciously is a vital skill for young individuals.*

i. *The Mirror to Your Brand: What Does Your Digital Presence Say?*

Before anyone meets you, they might "Google" you or check your social profiles. What impression are you leaving? Your digital presence is your personal brand – a sum total of how others perceive you online.

v. *Consistency is Key:*

Mismatch Mistake: If your online persona is vastly different from your real-life self (e.g., overly aggressive online, but meek in person), it creates dissonance and erodes trust.
Instead: Strive for authenticity and consistency. Your online self should be an accurate, if curated, reflection of your real values and personality.

v. *Purposeful Content Creation:*

Random Posting Mistake: Just sharing anything without thought or purpose.
Instead: Think about what you want your digital presence to convey. What are your passions? What unique insights do you have? What kind of value can you add to your network? Share content that aligns with your desired personal brand.
Example:

- *If you're passionate about fitness, share informed tips. If you love photography, showcase your best work. If you're a student, share insights on learning or college life.*

v.   *Quality Over Quantity:*

Spamming Mistake: Posting constantly with low-value content.
Instead: Focus on creating or sharing high-quality, thoughtful content. A few impactful posts are better than many irrelevant ones.

v.   *Leveraging Social Media for Positive Growth:*

Social media isn't just for entertainment; it can be a powerful tool for self-improvement and networking.

v.   *Learning & Skill Development:*

Follow Experts: Curate your feed to follow thought leaders, mentors, and experts in your areas of interest.

v.   *Online Courses & Tutorials: Platforms like YouTube, LinkedIn Learning, or specific educational apps offer a wealth of knowledge.*

v.   *Engage in Discussions: Participate in constructive discussions related to your field or interests.*
v.   *Networking & Community Building:*

Connect with Professionals: Use platforms like LinkedIn to connect with people in your desired industry.

v.   *Join Relevant Groups: Participate in online communities focused on your hobbies, career, or personal growth.*
v.   *Meaningful Engagement: Don't just "like" posts. Leave thoughtful comments, share valuable insights, and engage*

in genuine conversations.

v. *Showcasing Your Talents (Portfolio):*

For creative fields (design, writing, photography) or even just hobbies, social media can serve as a dynamic portfolio.

v. *Platforms: Instagram for visual arts, LinkedIn for professional achievements, YouTube for video content, personal blogs for writing.*
v. *Curate Carefully: Only showcase your best work.*
v. *Practicing Communication Skills:*

Social media offers a low-pressure environment to practice written communication, articulate thoughts concisely, and engage in respectful dialogue.

v. *Craft thoughtful replies: Take time to formulate clear, empathetic, and insightful responses.*
v. *Navigating the Pitfalls: Maintaining Well-being*

While powerful, social media has its downsides. Being mindful of these is crucial.

v. *Comparison Trap:*

Mistake: Constantly comparing your "behind-the-scenes" reality with others' "highlight reels."
Instead: Recognize that social media is often a curated version of reality. Focus on your own journey and progress. Limit exposure to accounts that trigger negative feelings.

v. *Time Sink & Distraction:*

Mistake: Mindless scrolling, letting social media eat into productive time.

Instead: Set time limits for social media use. Be intentional about why you're opening an app. Use it as a tool, not a time killer.

v.   *Negativity & Trolling:*

Mistake: Engaging in online arguments or letting negative comments affect you.

Instead: Protect your mental space. Don't feed the trolls. Learn to disengage, block, or mute accounts that drain your energy.

v.   *Privacy Concerns:*

Mistake: Oversharing personal information or not understanding privacy settings.

Instead: Be mindful of what you share publicly. Regularly check and adjust your privacy settings on all platforms.

By becoming a conscious architect of your digital presence, you transform social media from a potential distraction into a powerful asset. It allows you to express your evolving personality, connect with like-minded individuals, learn new skills, and expand your positive impact in the world. This strategic approach to growth is vital for handling life's inevitable challenges, which we'll discuss in the next chapter.

CHAPTER XIV

The Resilience Blueprint: Turning Setbacks into Comebacks

"It's not how many times you fall, but how many times you get up." - Abraham Lincoln

You've built your inner foundations, honed your social skills, and mastered your digital presence. But here's an undeniable truth: life will throw challenges your way. Exams will be tough, relationships might falter, career paths will have detours, and self-doubt may occasionally creep back in. The measure of your transformation isn't the absence of problems, but your ability to navigate them. This is the Resilience Blueprint – the ability to bounce back from adversity, learn from setbacks, and turn potential defeats into powerful comebacks.

In Indian society, where pressure to succeed (academically, professionally) can be intense, developing resilience is not just a personal trait but a survival skill. It's about enduring *hardship and emerging stronger.*

i. *Understanding Resilience: More Than Just "Toughness"*

Resilience isn't about being immune to pain or never feeling discouraged. It's about:

v. *Adaptability: Adjusting to change and new circumstances.*
v. *Problem-Solving: Actively seeking solutions rather than dwelling on problems.*
v. *Emotional Regulation: Managing difficult emotions without letting them overwhelm you (revisiting Chapter 2).*
v. *Optimism: Maintaining a positive outlook, even in challenging times.*
v. *Self-Compassion: Being kind to yourself during setbacks, rather than overly self-critical.*

The Three Pillars of Your Resilience Blueprint:

v. *Mindset: The Power of Perspective (Revisited CBT)*

Your initial reaction to a setback often determines your ability to recover. Resilience starts in your mind.

v. *Challenge Catastrophizing: When something goes wrong, our mind often jumps to the worst-case scenario ("I failed that exam, now my whole career is over!").*

Instead: Use CBT techniques (from Chapter 2 & 3). Ask: "Is this thought 100% true? What's the evidence? What's a more realistic perspective?"

v. *The Growth Mindset (Carol Dweck): Believe that your abilities and intelligence can be developed through dedication and hard work. A setback isn't a permanent judgment of your ability, but an opportunity to learn and improve.*

Fixed Mindset: "I failed, I'm not smart enough."
Growth Mindset: "I failed, what can I learn from this to do better next time?"

Exercise:

- *Reframe the Setback. Think of a recent disappointment or failure. How did you initially react? Now, reframe it using a growth mindset. What lesson can you extract? What action can you take based on that lesson?*

v. *Emotional Regulation & Self-Care:*

Resilient individuals allow themselves to feel negative emotions but don't let them fester indefinitely. They actively engage in self-care.

v. *Acknowledge and Process: Don't suppress feelings of disappointment, anger, or sadness. Acknowledge them, feel them, and then actively process them through healthy outlets (journaling, talking to a trusted friend, exercise).*
v. *Prioritize Physical Well-being: When stressed, it's easy to neglect sleep, nutrition, and exercise. But these are precisely when your body and mind need them most (revisit Chapter 5).*
v. *Mindfulness & Meditation: Even short bursts of mindfulness can help you stay grounded and observe your*

thoughts without getting swept away by them during challenging times.

Exercise:

• *Your "Crisis" Self-Care Kit. What are 3-5 quick, healthy activities you can do when you feel overwhelmed by a setback? (e.g., a 10-minute walk, calling a supportive friend, listening to calming music, deep breathing). Have this list ready.*

v. *Action & Problem-Solving:*

Resilience isn't passive acceptance; it's active engagement with the problem.

v. *Focus on What You Can Control: In any difficult situation, identify the things within your control and focus your energy there. Release what you cannot control.*

v. *Solution-Oriented Thinking: Instead of dwelling on the problem, shift your focus to potential solutions. Brainstorm ideas, even if they seem small.*

v. *Seek Support (Wisely): Don't be afraid to ask for help from mentors, friends, family, or professionals. This is a sign of strength, not weakness. In Indian families, seeking advice from elders or close family members is often a key support mechanism.*

v. *Small Steps Forward: Just like conquering procrastination (Chapter 4), break down the problem into the smallest possible actionable steps. Even a tiny step forward creates momentum and reduces feelings of helplessness.*

Exercise:

- *The "Post-Setback Action Plan."*

Acknowledge the Emotion: "I feel [emotion] about [setback]."

Extract the Lesson: "What did I learn from this? What could I do differently next time?"

Identify Actionable Steps: List 1-3 concrete, small steps you can take today or tomorrow to address the situation or move forward.

v. *The Power of Narrative: Your Comeback Story*

Every setback is an opportunity to write a powerful comeback story. How you frame the challenge, how you respond to it, and the lessons you extract become part of your personal narrative. By consciously choosing a narrative of resilience and growth, you empower yourself to face any storm and emerge stronger. This continuous journey of growth and adaptation is what we'll explore in our final chapter.

CHAPTER XV

The Perpetual Flame: Sustaining Your Transformed Life

"Growth is never by mere chance; it is the result of forces working together." - James Cash Penney

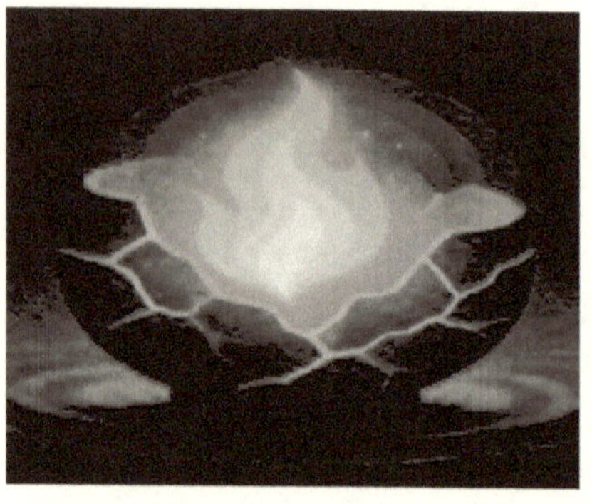

You've ignited the flame within. You've built self-awareness, mastered emotions, cultivated confidence, conquered procrastination, optimized your physical well-being, enhanced your charisma and communication, deepened your understanding of relationships, leveraged humor, refined your image, designed your digital presence, and built resilience. This is a monumental achievement. But transformation isn't a destination; it's a continuous journey. This final chapter, The Perpetual Flame, is about establishing the habits, mindsets, and systems that ensure your growth is sustainable, your inner flame never extinguishes, and you continue to evolve into the *best version of yourself, every single day.*

In India, the concept of lifelong learning and self-improvement (often rooted in spiritual and philosophical traditions) aligns perfectly with the idea of a "perpetual flame." It's about conscious living and continuous refinement.

i. *The Habits of Sustained Growth: Building Your Support System*

To maintain your transformed self, you need structures and practices that reinforce your positive changes.

v. *Continuous Self-Reflection & Journaling:*

Why it's important: Prevents you from slipping back into old patterns. Allows you to track progress, identify new challenges, and celebrate wins.

Practice: Continue your thought and emotional journals. Set aside 10-15 minutes each week to reflect on:
What went well this week?
What challenges did I face, and how did I handle them?
What did I learn?
What is one small thing I want to improve next week?

v. *Regular Skill Practice & Learning:*

Why it's important: Stagnation is the enemy of growth. The world evolves, and so should you.

Practice: Actively seek new knowledge. Read books, take online courses, learn a new language, practice a new skill related to your field or hobby. Continuously refine your communication and social skills through real-world application.

v.   *Maintain Your Physical & Mental Well-being Rituals:*

Why it's important: These are your foundational energy sources. Neglecting them will quickly erode your progress.

Practice: Consistently adhere to your sleep schedule, nutritious eating habits, and regular movement. Schedule time for mindfulness, meditation, or quiet reflection. Make these non-negotiable parts of your routine.

v.   *Nurture Your Support Network:*

Why it's important: You don't have to do it alone. Surrounding yourself with positive, supportive individuals (friends, family, mentors) provides encouragement, perspective, and accountability.

Practice: Regularly connect with your trusted circle. Offer support as well as receive it. Seek out mentors who inspire you. In India, valuing and maintaining family and community bonds is a strength to leverage.

v.   *Set New, Empowering Goals:*

Why it's important: Goals provide direction and purpose. Once you achieve one, set another. This keeps you motivated and engaged.

Practice: Review your values (Chapter 1) and set short-term (3-6 months) and long-term (1-3 years) goals that align with them. Make them SMART (Specific, Measurable, Achievable, Relevant, Time-bound).

v.   *Embracing Imperfection: The Realism of Growth*

No one is perfect, and growth is rarely linear. There will be days when you feel less motivated, when you stumble, or when old habits try to creep back in.

v.   *Self-Compassion: Be kind to yourself during these times. Don't let a minor slip become a full relapse. Acknowledge it, learn from it, and get back on track.*

v.   *Progress, Not Perfection: Celebrate small victories. Focus on consistent effort over flawless execution.*
v.   *Flexibility: Life happens. Be adaptable. If a strategy isn't working, adjust it. If a goal needs to change, change it.*
v.   *Your Legacy: Inspiring Others*

As you continue to ignite your own flame, you will inevitably inspire those around you. Your journey of self-improvement isn't just for you; it has a ripple effect. By living authentically, confidently, and with purpose, you become a beacon for others, demonstrating what's possible.

v.   *Mentor and Guide: As you gain experience, consider sharing your knowledge and insights with others who are just starting their own journeys.*

v.   *Lead by Example: **Your actions will speak louder than any words.** Be the change you wish to see.*

The perpetual flame is fueled by consistent effort, genuine self-care, a growth mindset, and the courage to keep learning and evolving. This isn't the end of your journey; it's just the beginning of a life lived with intentionality, confidence, and unending potential. Your fire, now unleashed, will light your way forward.

Conclusion: Your Fire, Unleashed – The Journey Continues

You've reached the final pages of "Ignite: Rise from Within," but this is not an ending. It is a powerful new beginning. Throughout these chapters, we've embarked on a transformative journey together:

We began by becoming the Inner Architect, meticulously mapping your thoughts, emotions, and values to build a solid foundation of self-awareness. You learned to be an Emotional Alchemist, transforming raw feelings into fuel for growth and mastering your inner world with grace. We then initiated a Mindset Reset, cultivating unbreakable confidence by challenging limiting beliefs and harnessing the power of affirmations and visualization. You broke Beyond the Wall of procrastination, activating your drive and momentum through strategic action. We then fueled your engine with Physical Ignite, optimizing your body through sleep, nutrition, and movement, recognizing its profound link to your mental power.

Moving into the social sphere, you unleashed your Charisma, learning the art of magnetic presence. You became a Master Connector, honing superior communication and social fluency. We then delved into Decoding Her World, understanding female psychology to build genuine connections, and applied this knowledge through the Attraction Playbook to spark authentic chemistry. You learned to be a Modern "Playmaker," sustaining interest and charm beyond the initial spark.

Finally, we integrated these transformations into your broader life: You embraced Humor & Wit as your social superpower, enhancing every interaction. You became an Image Architect, aligning your external presentation with your internal power. We navigated your Digital Presence, leveraging social media for positive impact and personal branding. You forged your Resilience Blueprint, learning to turn every setback into a powerful comeback. And now, you stand ready to cultivate The Perpetual Flame, ensuring your growth is continuous and your transformed life is sustainable.

This book has provided you with a comprehensive toolkit. It's not a magic wand, but a guide to the consistent effort and conscious practice that will lead to profound, lasting change. Remember, the journey of self-mastery is an ongoing one. There will be new challenges, new lessons, and new versions of yourself waiting to be discovered.

The most crucial takeaway is this: The power to transform, to connect, and to thrive has always resided within you. This book simply offered the map and the strategies to access that power. You have the inner fire. It's time to keep it burning brightly, not just for yourself, but for the positive impact you will undoubtedly have on the world around you.

Go forth, live your life with purpose, connect with authenticity, and never stop igniting the extraordinary potential that is uniquely yours. Your fire is unleashed. The journey continues.

www.ingramcontent.com/pod-product-compliance
Lightning Source LLC
Chambersburg PA
CBHW020604160726
47991CB00002B/865